Table of Contents

For a free printable PDF and playable Musescore page, go to:

https://sites.google.com/view/drum-book-by-nozomi/home

Introduction

About This Book: Drum Crash Course

This book provides a concise overview of the invaluable insights I've gained throughout my years as a dedicated drummer and educator. Its primary focus is to help you grasp fundamental skills in playing drums. The book's structure mirrors the process of developing essential skills and their practical use. Whether followed sequentially or as a topic-based reference guide, the design adapts to your learning preferences. I hope that with this book you'll feel confident in your fundamentals while discovering areas that are most interesting to you.

For All Levels: Beginner to Experienced

Whether you're a beginner or experienced, the appendix links offer valuable technique insights. I suggest beginning your journey there to ensure your technique is solid. Practicing good technique lets you accomplish challenges while minimizing strain - drumming is a physically active art!

Things to Remember When Playing:

• **Practice slow to play fast:** if you want to rock those lightning-fast solos, start by practicing at a snail's pace. It might sound counterintuitive, but taking it slow actually trains your muscles and brain to nail those speedy rhythms with ease.

• **Metronomes are your friend:** Metronomes help you develop your own internal timing. This is important whether you're playing along to your favorite track or playing with others. Having good timing is the core of being a good musician, especially a drummer.

• **Inhale, Exhale, Drum:** Drummers often hold their breath while playing—an all too common habit. Correcting this tendency can enhance your experience and performance. Try it out, and you'll likely feel and play better.

• **Most importantly, have fun!**

Gratitude to Generous Contributors

Huge thank you to these incredible people who helped me on this immense endeavor:

Rose Nguyễn - I am so grateful for your enthusiasm, knowledge, and motivational push. Your review and editing notes of the book hold a significance beyond words. Thank you so much.

Emily Mar - Thank you so much for taking the time to design the book cover. It made me tear up when I saw it, as your expertise being poured into it made me feel incredibly supported.

Matthew Kusche - You were the first person to see the whole book and I was terrified because you're a great drummer and have experience teaching! Your approval boosted my confidence. Thank you.

I want to express my gratitude to Brittany for her positive impact on my life. Thank you for combing through this book. You're an amazing colleague, student, and friend.

Thank you to my wonderful students. I feel honored to spend time with such remarkable individuals who share my passion. Thank you for having me as your teacher.

My kind and patient husband, Carl. Thank you for your support through this daunting but rewarding experience.

I am so lucky to have you all in my life. I could not have done this without you!

Notation

Drum notation key:

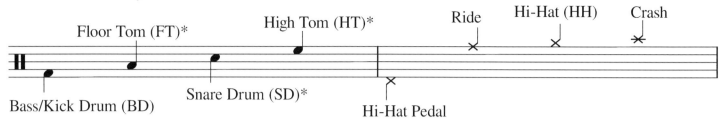

*The stem of the snare and the toms can be up or down. In this book, we will see both so you can get used to them.

Below are notes and their American English name, how many beats they're worth, as well as relevant rests. Rests are crucial for the timing of when to play a note.

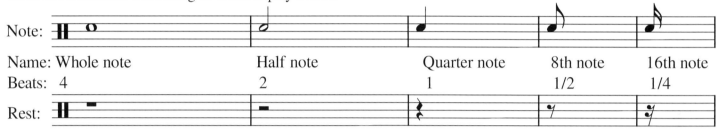

Name:	Whole note	Half note	Quarter note	8th note	16th note
Beats:	4	2	1	1/2	1/4

Below you will see 4/4 at the start of the measure, which is a time signature. A time signature tells you how to count the beats so your timing is correct. 4/4 means there are four quarter notes per measure. The bottom number is what we're counting, in this case, quarter notes. The top number is how many, in this case, 4. This can also be represented with a "C," short for "common time." A lot of popular music is in 4/4. Later, we will explore other frequently used time signatures such as 3/4 (3 quarter notes in a measure), 6/8 (6 eighth notes in a measure), as well as "odd" ones. The symbol "+" is used to represent "and," enhancing readability and speed in notation, compared to the more complex "and" or "&" alternatives. Let's visualize the different note values in a 4/4 measure.

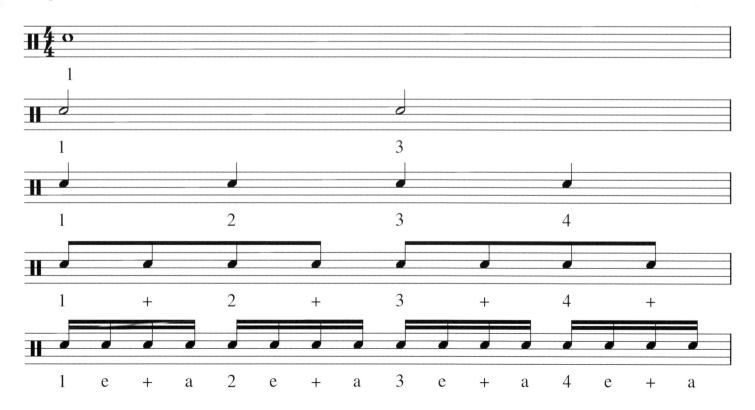

Learning Rhythms

Using words we are familiar with can help with learning rhythms. This exercise is best done with an instructor or with a metronome.

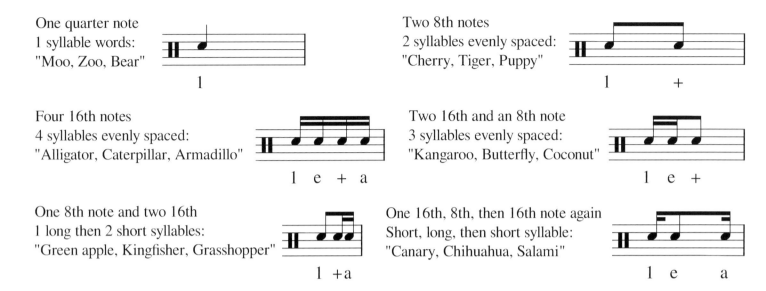

One quarter note
1 syllable words:
"Moo, Zoo, Bear"

1

Two 8th notes
2 syllables evenly spaced:
"Cherry, Tiger, Puppy"

1   +

Four 16th notes
4 syllables evenly spaced:
"Alligator, Caterpillar, Armadillo"

1   e   +   a

Two 16th and an 8th note
3 syllables evenly spaced:
"Kangaroo, Butterfly, Coconut"

1   e   +

One 8th note and two 16th
1 long then 2 short syllables:
"Green apple, Kingfisher, Grasshopper"

1   +a

One 16th, 8th, then 16th note again
Short, long, then short syllable:
"Canary, Chihuahua, Salami"

1   e   a

"Sticking" refers to which limb plays a specific part. Abbreviations you'll see for sticking:
RH = Right Hand   LH = Left Hand   RF = Right Foot   LF = Left Foot
Reverse these if playing on a left-handed drum set (hi-hat is to your right).

A good way to practice is to play one drum at a time.
Try playing the cymbal first then add the bass/snare in.
If the hi hat is too tricky, start with the ride cymbal.

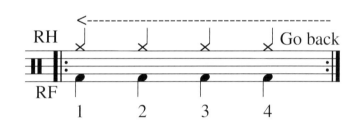

The two dots at the end of the measure are a repeat
mark. The dots make a sandwich of what to repeat.
The dots to the right of the lines is where you go back
to when you get to the dots left of the lines.

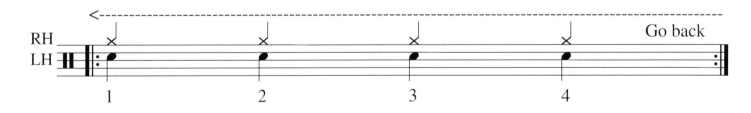

If you're struggling with what notes are played together, you can
use something to cover the majority of the measure and uncover
as you go. I like to use sticky notes. You can also use a highlighter
to highlight each count.

4

Many drum beats have the bass drum play on beats 1 and 3, and the snare drum on beats 2 and 4.
Once you feel comfortable playing the first line, try adding the hi-hat/ride.

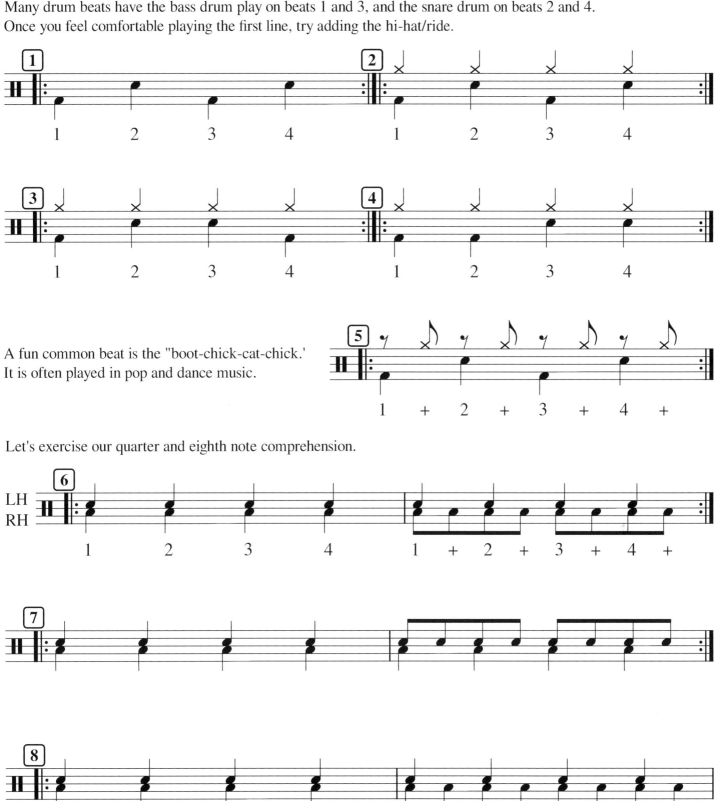

A fun common beat is the "boot-chick-cat-chick."
It is often played in pop and dance music.

Let's exercise our quarter and eighth note comprehension.

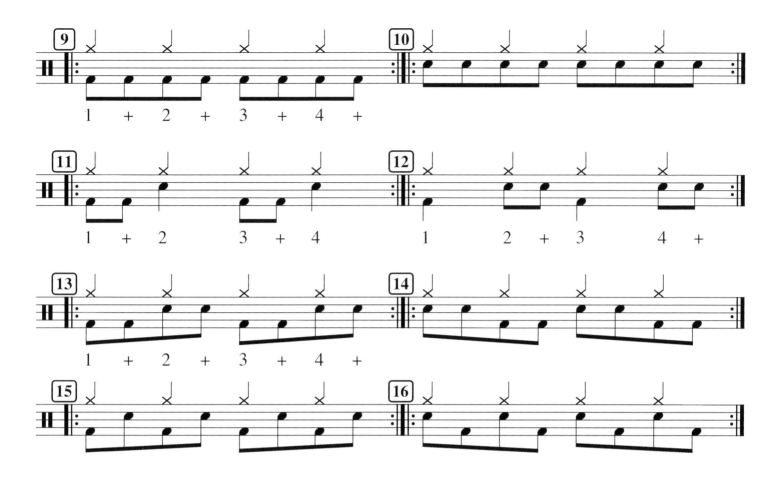

Let's play some eighth note hi-hats! We'll start with the same basic beat. As you can see below, the only difference between the two is that you are playing on the "and" ("+" symbol) with the hi-hat.

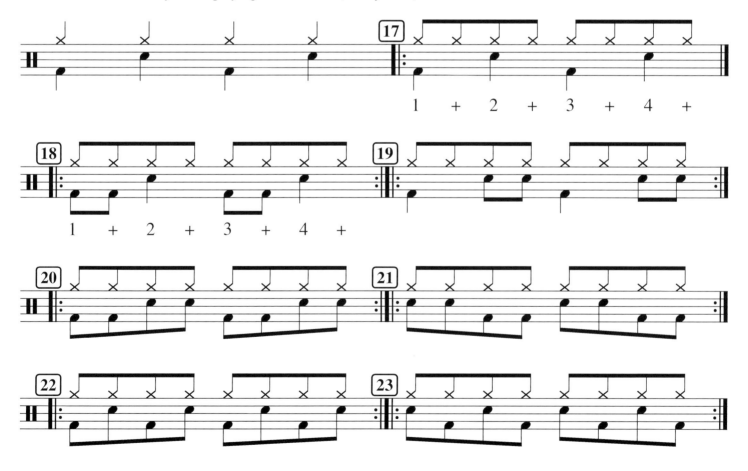

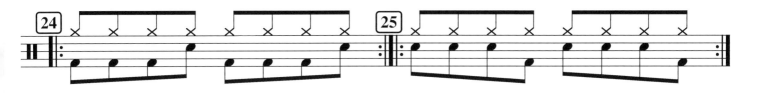

Let's work on some trickier beats with both quarter note and eighth note hi-hats.

Building Chops: Rudiments PT1

We will do a deeper dive into rudiments later. For now, let's focus on a few fundamentals to get you started. In this chapter, we will also start discussing dynamics.

Single Stroke Roll

Double Stroke Roll

For stronger doubles, we will practice accenting the second note. What does that mean? An accented note, notated by ">," means to emphasize the note. Basically, play louder. In order to do the following exercise effectively, it helps to know stroke types.

• Full Stroke (F) - Start and end with stick in the up position. You can think of the up position as the stick tip about a foot away from the drum head.

• Down Stroke (D) - Start in the up position then end with down. The down position is when the stick tip is a few inches (or less) from the drum head.

• Tap Stroke (T) - Starts and ends in the down position.

• Up Stroke (U) - Starts with the down position and ends with the up position.

Practice the following strokes on each hand.

Let's get those strong doubles!

Let's add the feet for four way coordination.

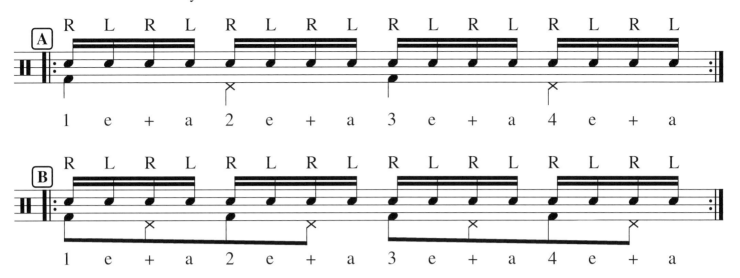

Level up: try the above exercises with double stroke rolls.

Time to move around the drums! Play single strokes for the following. When it's easy, add feet.

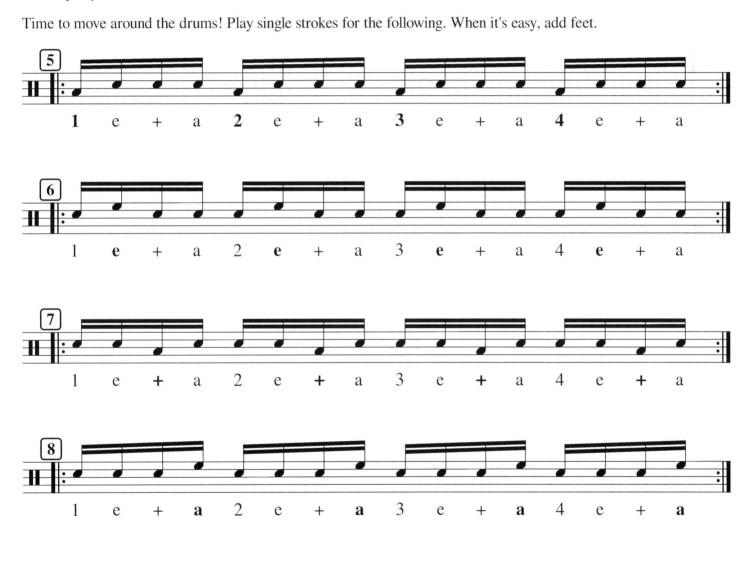

9

Let's turn these rudiments into fills.

Single Stroke Roll

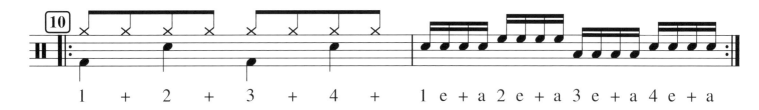

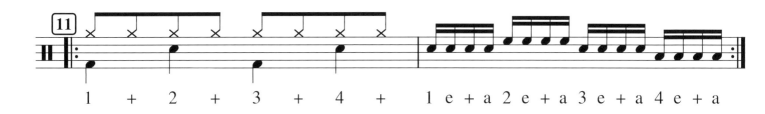

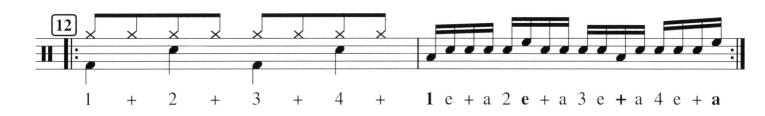

Double Stroke Roll

Transcribing

Transcribing is when you write down what you hear in a piece of music. It can be handy for learning your favorite songs. Some songs are more challenging, not just the parts being more complicated, but also how the song was recorded. The drums might be too quiet or have lots of reverb, making it difficult to hear. Some recordings are layered, which means there are multiple recordings of the drums on top of each other. This can make it impossible to play.

I tackle transcribing by listening for the most prominent parts and counting. Often it is the snare and hi-hat. The bass drum can be hard to hear, but I often feel it in my chest (corny, but it works!). Writing the count can help too. I write what I hear, then play it back. It's better to play too little than too much. Overplaying can make it hard to hear what's happening. Watching live versions of a song can help to see what the drummer is doing. Drum cover videos help as well. Start by just listening; if you're stuck, you can watch the player to see which drums they are hitting.

It can be tough to replicate other drummers perfectly, so don't worry about playing the exact same thing. If it fits the music well, that's the most important part! Pick a song that has easily audible drums and use the blank measures below to try transcribing.

The next two pages have 16th note counts included below the staff, so you can count and write notes easier.

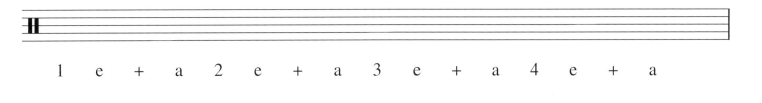

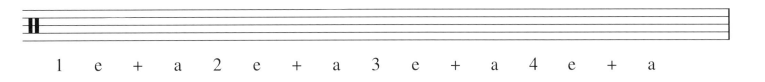

Staff 1

1 e + a 2 e + a 3 e + a 4 e + a   1 e + a 2 e + a 3 e + a 4 e + a

Staff 2

1 e + a 2 e + a 3 e + a 4 e + a   1 e + a 2 e + a 3 e + a 4 e + a

Staff 3

1 e + a 2 e + a 3 e + a 4 e + a   1 e + a 2 e + a 3 e + a 4 e + a

Staff 4

1 e + a 2 e + a 3 e + a 4 e + a   1 e + a 2 e + a 3 e + a 4 e + a

Staff 5

1 e + a 2 e + a 3 e + a 4 e + a   1 e + a 2 e + a 3 e + a 4 e + a

Staff 6

1 e + a 2 e + a 3 e + a 4 e + a   1 e + a 2 e + a 3 e + a 4 e + a

Half Time/Double Time

These are fun and useful tools to have in your pocket. You can completely change the feeling of a song by using these. Double time will make everything upbeat. Half time will feel more groovy.

Back beat (snare on 2 and 4)

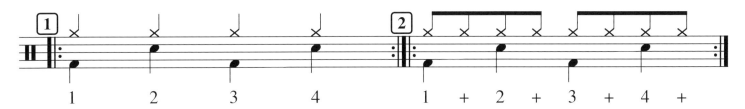

Half time

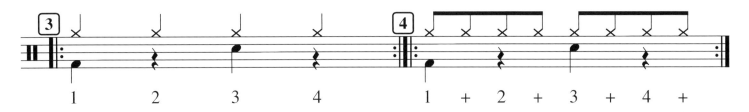

Double time

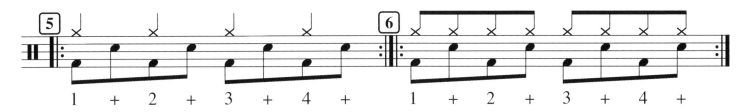

Let's practice back and forth.

Adding Crash

The crash can be used to highlight any part of a beat. It is most commonly used to accent the 1 of a new section. It can also be used instead of the hi-hat for a beat, typically in rock music. The bass or snare drum is often played at the same time to pack an extra punch.

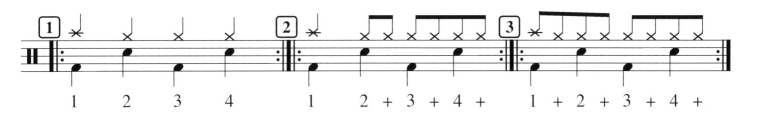

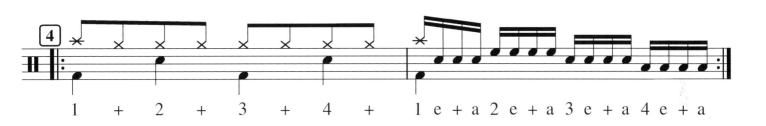

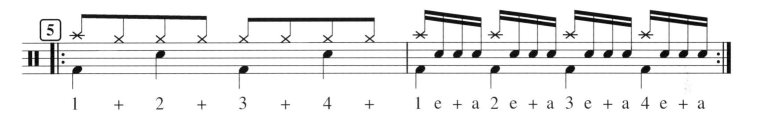

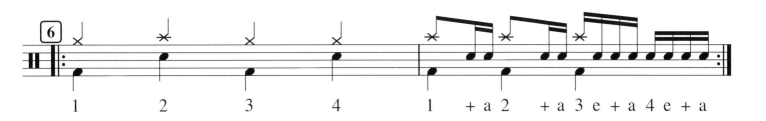

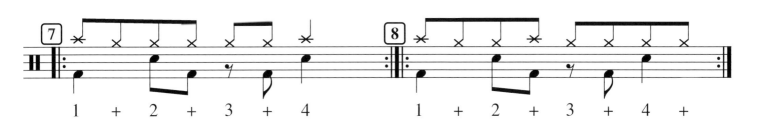

Let's add the crash to some half time/double time exercises.

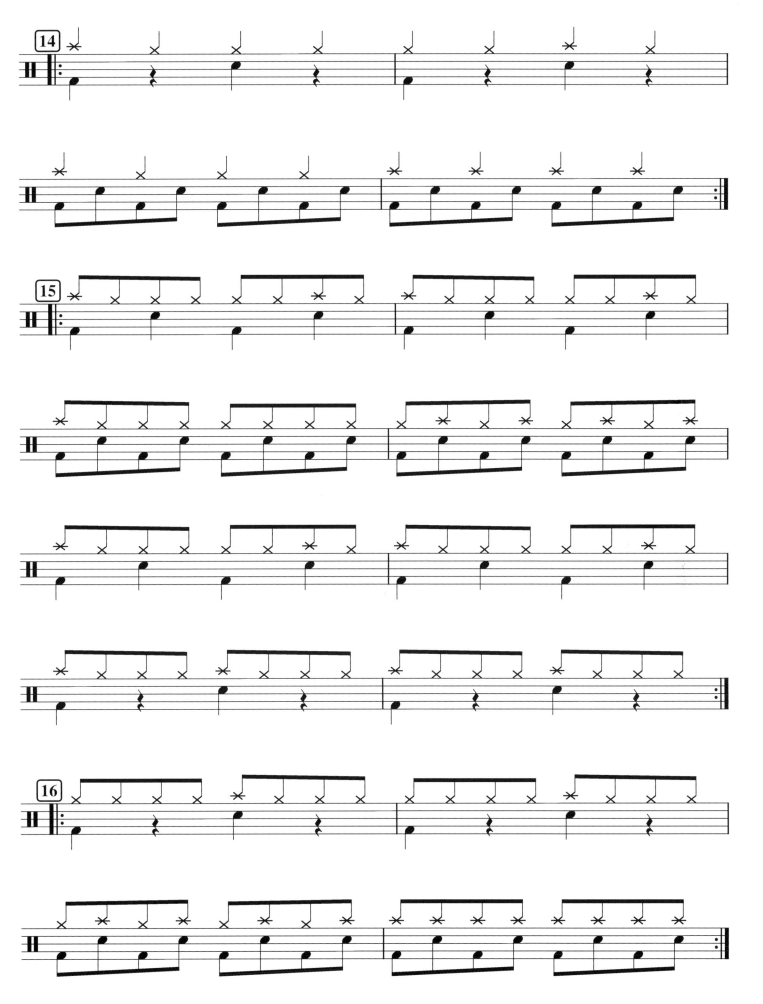

Alternating 16th Note Hi-Hats

The following two pages are designed to help you with your coordination and understanding of 16th note placements.

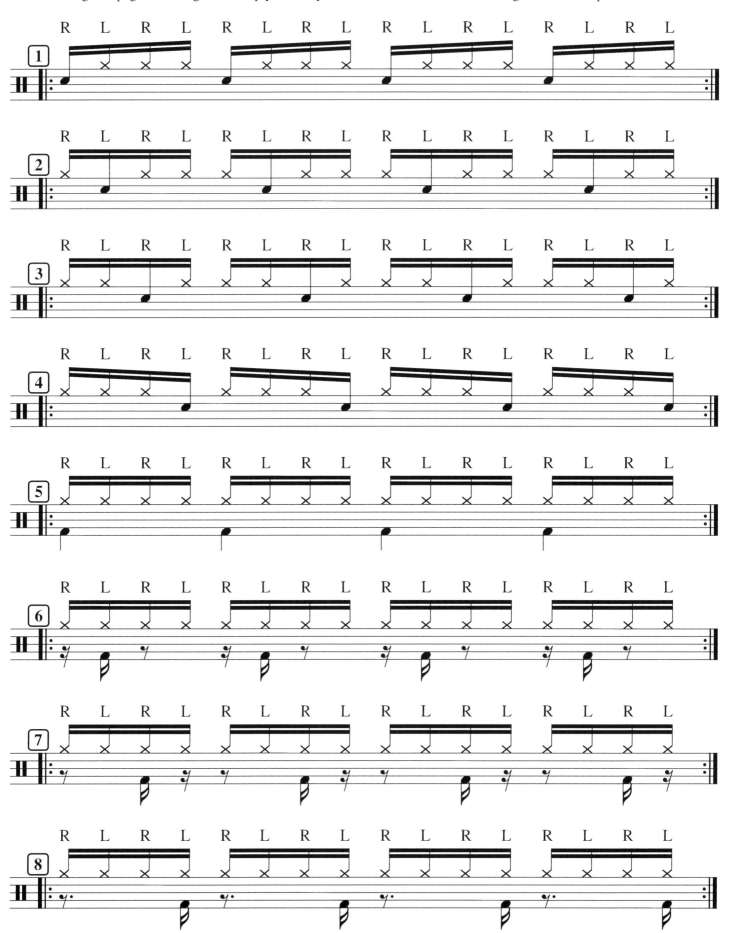

Let's play some grooves!

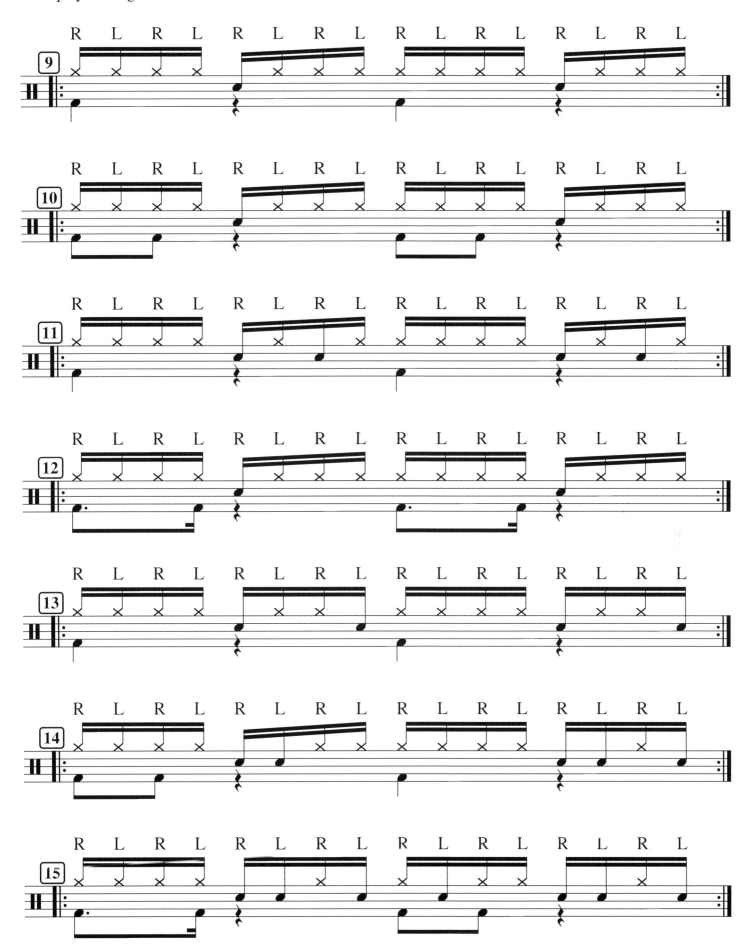

16th Note Grooves

Practicing the following exercises will help you develop your 16th note bass and snare drum rhythms.

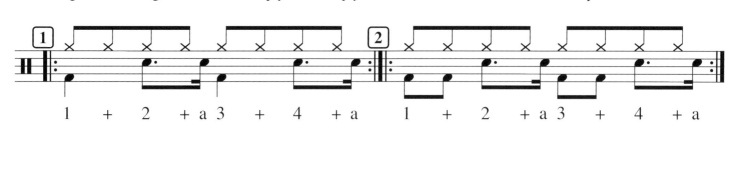

1 + 2 + a 3 + 4 + a   1 + 2 + a 3 + 4 + a

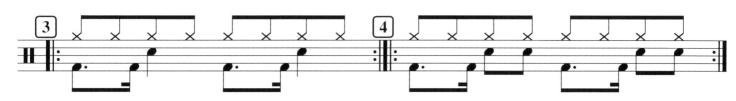

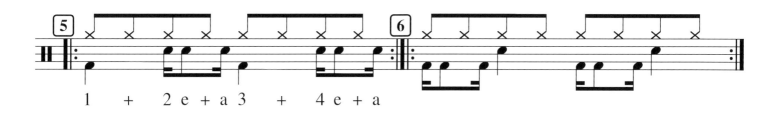

1 + 2 e + a 3 + 4 e + a

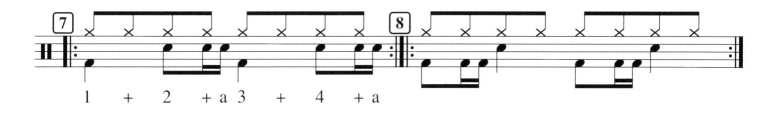

1 + 2 + a 3 + 4 + a

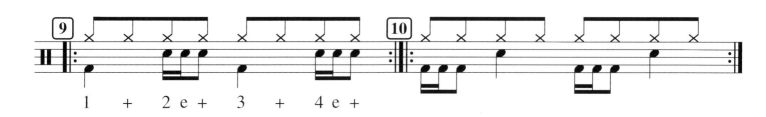

1 + 2 e + 3 + 4 e +

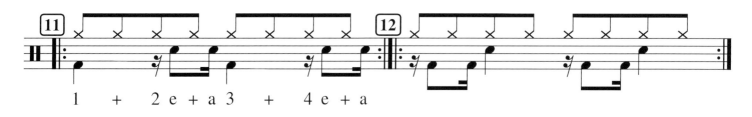

1 + 2 e + a 3 + 4 e + a

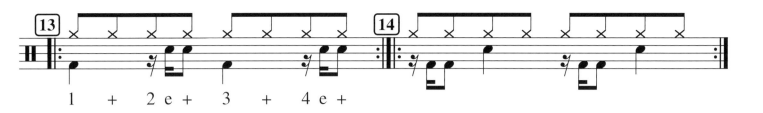

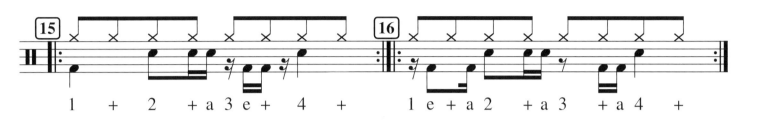

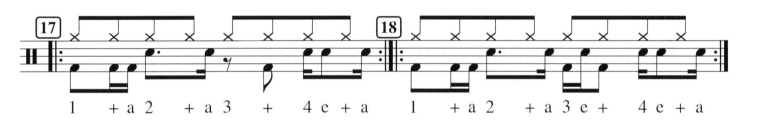

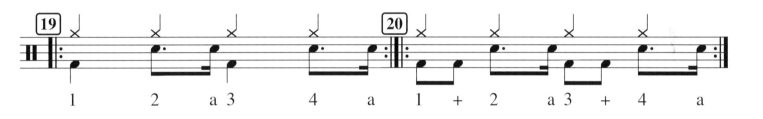

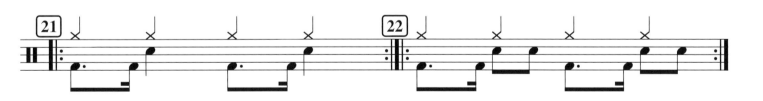

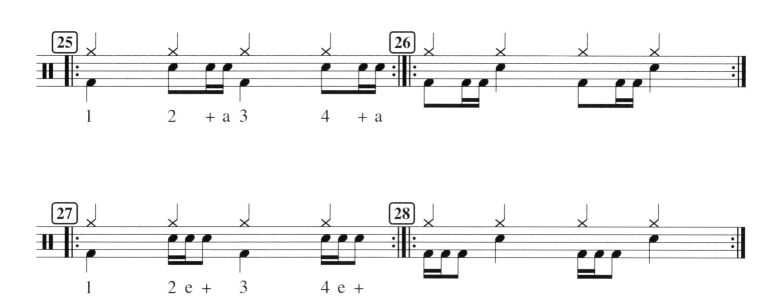

1   2   + a 3   4   + a

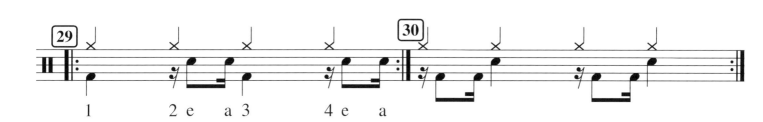

1   2 e + 3   4 e +

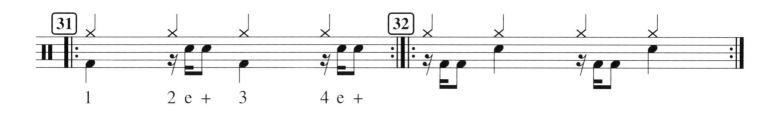

1   2 e a 3   4 e a

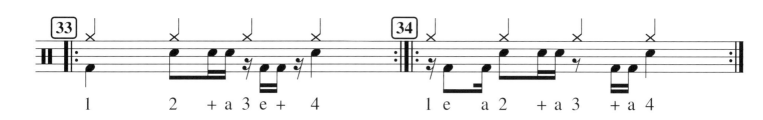

1   2 e + 3   4 e +

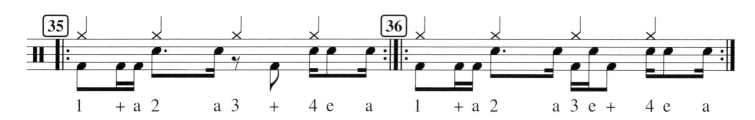

1 + a 2   a 3 + 4 e a   1 + a 2   a 3 e + 4 e a

Dynamics

Dynamics are critical for music. They can make the same notes feel completely different.

Below are four common dynamic marks from soft to loud:

p is short for "piano," meaning "soft"

m is short for "mezzo," meaning "medium"

mp is short for "mezzo-piano," meaning "medium-soft"

mf is short for "mezzo-forte," meaning "medium-loud"

f is short for "forte," meaning "loud"

When going from soft to loud gradually, it is called "crescendo." "Crescendo" can be noted in the following two ways:

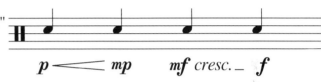

When going from loud to soft, it is called "decrescendo" or "diminuendo." Typically, when using letters to notate, "dim" is used. However, you may also see it written as "decresc."

Open Hi-Hat

Open hi-hats are notated with a "○" above the hi-hat note. We will see another use of "+", which is for a closed hi-hat. If you do not see any notation above, it is closed. This may vary depending on the author, but there is often a notation key provided.

We will first warm up by getting comfortable with using the hi-hat pedal. Make sure to use those core muscles!

Warm up:

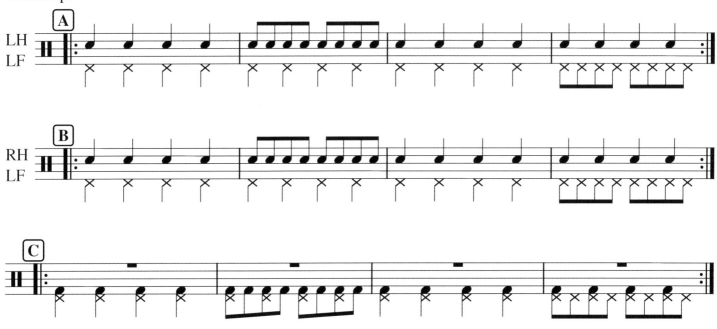

Let's get into four-way coordination.

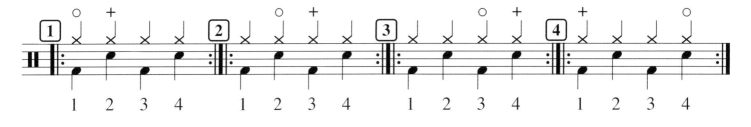

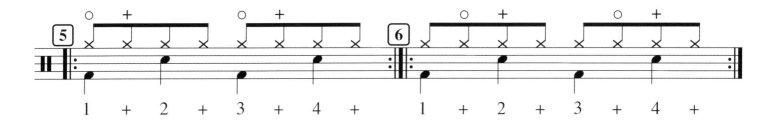

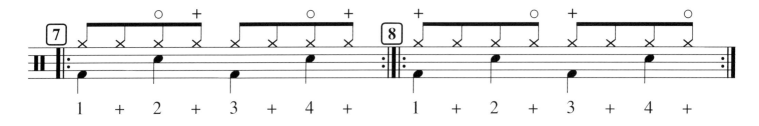

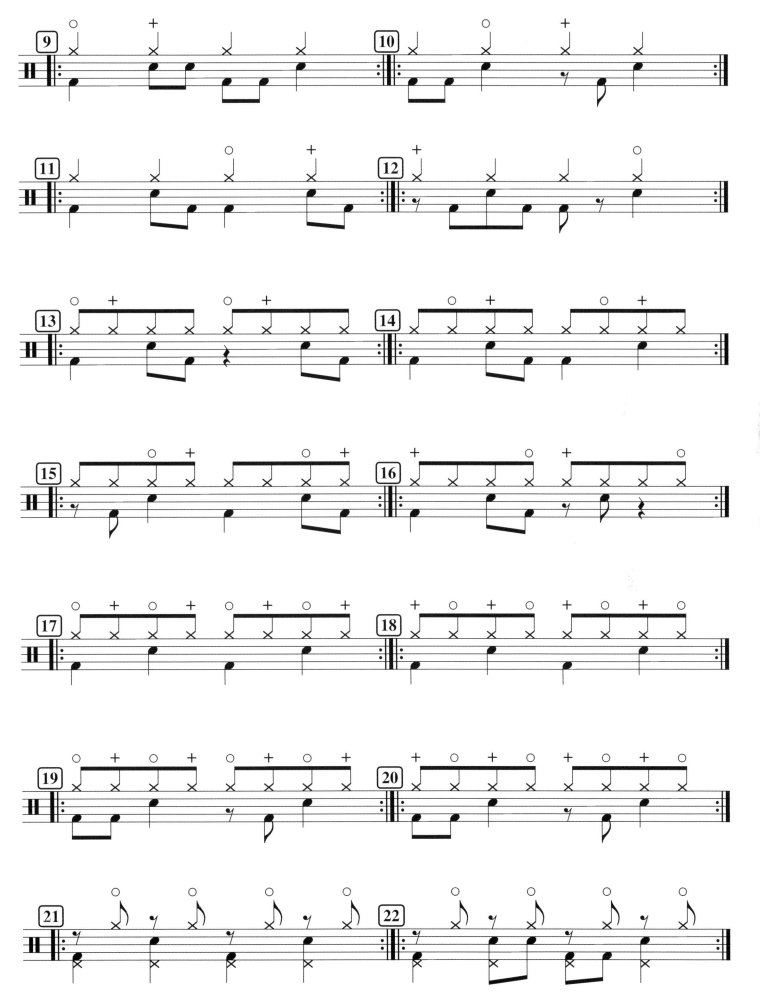

Application PT1

Now for the fun part – applying the exercises we've mastered to play a dynamic song structure with beats and fills.

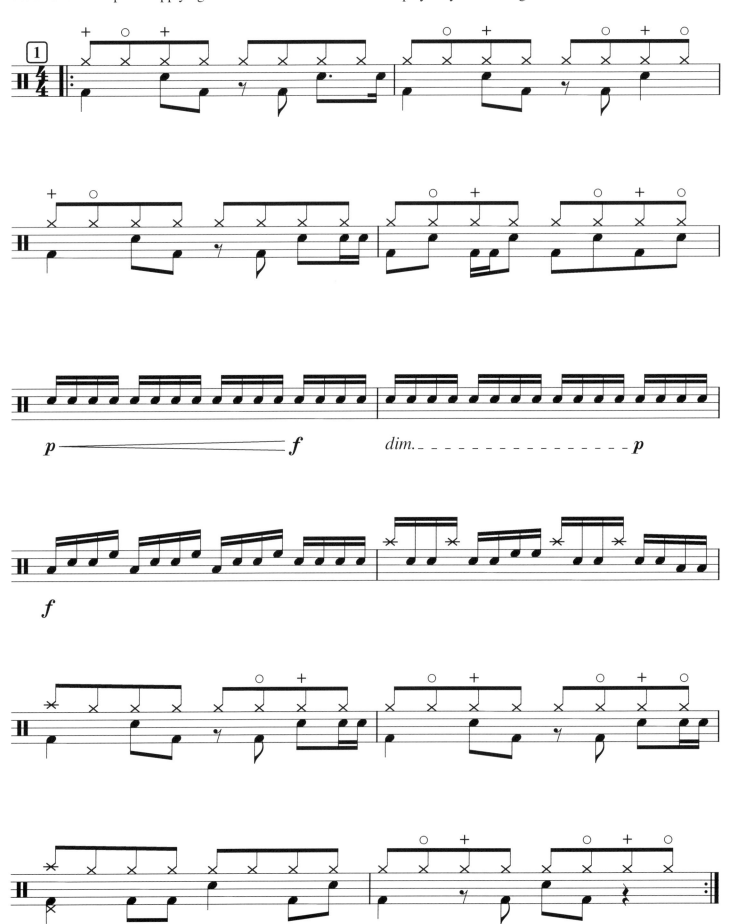

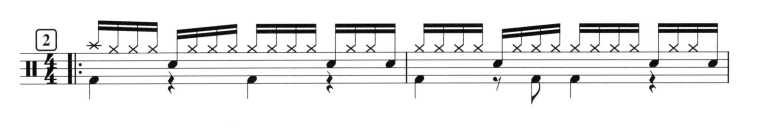

Triplets

When three notes are evenly played in the space of two, we call these triplets. Below, we have the regular note values followed by the triplets. With a metronome, go back and forth between the regular notes and the triplets.

8th Note Triplets

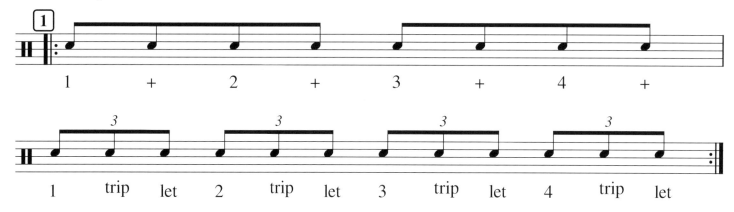

16th Note Triplets

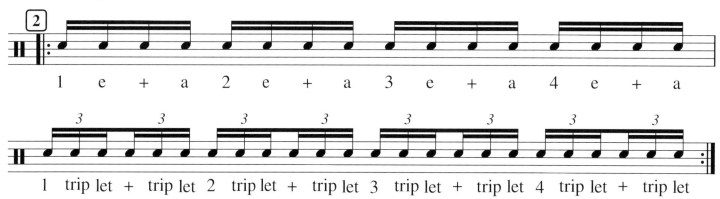

Quarter Note Triplets can be trickier. The (*italic*) words are placeholder counts. Saying them out loud can help with spacing but don't play them. You can also drum alternating 8th note triplets, but air drum with your left hand to hear your right hand play the quarter note triplets.

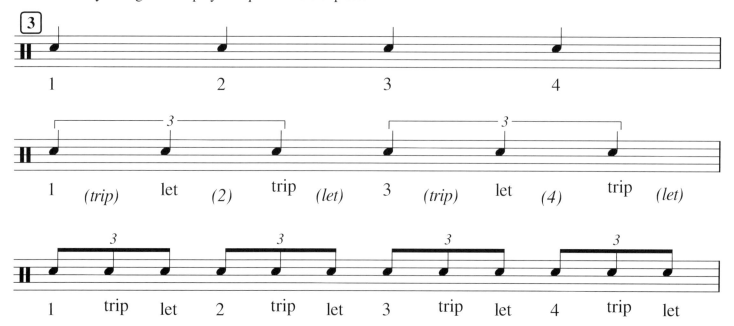

Triplet Fills

Being able to transition between 16th notes and 8th note triplets sounds super cool when playing fills. The following exercises are designed to help you feel comfortable with these versatile rhythmic textures.

Once you've established the feel of playing triplets, elevate your performance by incorporating the following dynamics into the previous fills.

Practice just the hands first, then add the feet.

If you breezed through the previous workout and smoothly blended it into your solo, why not give the next exercise a try? Spice up your solos with some 16th note triplets – you got this!

16th Note Triplet Grooves

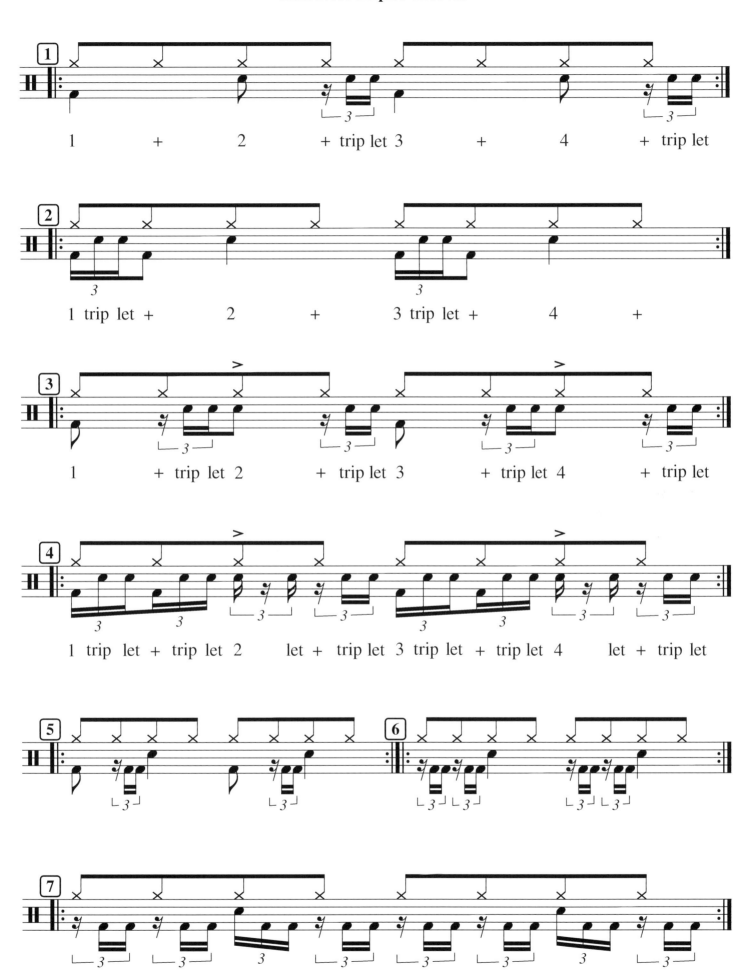

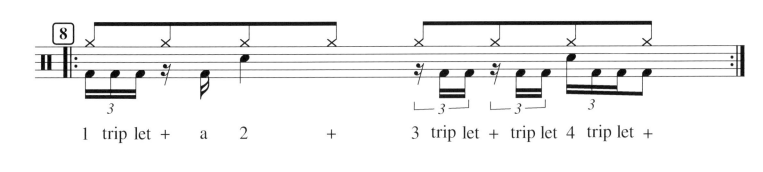

1 trip let + a 2 + 3 trip let + trip let 4 trip let +

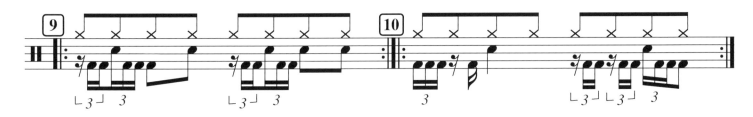

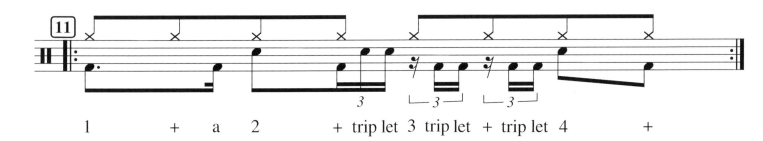

1 + a 2 + trip let 3 trip let + trip let 4 +

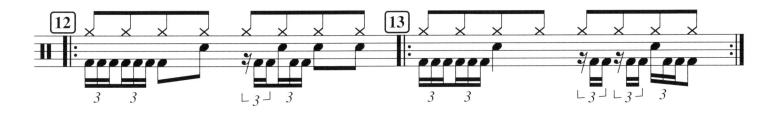

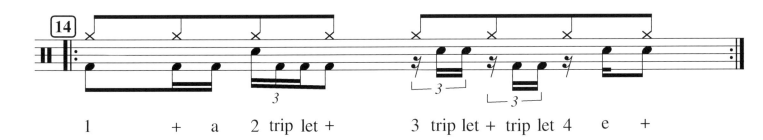

1 + a 2 trip let + 3 trip let + trip let 4 e +

Half time shuffle inspired by the Purdie shuffle.

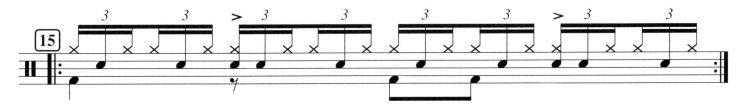

Building Chops: Rudiments PT2

Rudiments are great for developing speed and accuracy in your playing. They are the building blocks of drumming, and without them you wouldn't be able to play much! There's even a list called the 40 essential rudiments. These are especially great for practicing when you don't have a drum set. You can play these as fills or create fun grooves out of them. We won't cover all 40 in this book. I recommend using the resources provided to learn them all. I like the web page provided by the Percussive Arts Society. The link is provided in the appendix.

For these exercises, start with right-hand leading then left-hand leading. If you're a lefty, since we will be doing both stickings, you don't have to flip stickings for the following section.

Single Stroke Rolls

R L R L R L R L R L R L R L R L   L R L R L R L R L R L R L R L R

Double Stroke Rolls

R R L L R R L L R R L L R R L L   L L R R L L R R L L R R L L R R

Paradiddle

R L R R L R L L R L R R L R L L

L R L L R L R R L R L L R L R R

Once comfortable, add the feet in as we have in pt1 for all of the rudiments.

33

Double Paradiddle

R L R L R R L R L R L L R L R R   L L R L R R L L R L L R R L R

Single Paradiddle-diddle

R L R R L L R L R R L L   L R L L R R L R L L R R

Slash Notation

A slash through the stem means you play half of the note value for the duration of the note. So, one slash would be half of the note value played twice. Two slashes would be a quarter of the note value played four times. Three would be a sixteenth of the note value played eight times. With enough practice, you'll recognize the rhythms and won't need to think about this. Lucky for us, a lot of rolls have a number on top to show how many notes will be played. For example:

A quarter note with one slash means you play two eighth notes. Multiply the bottom number by 2 to get the value: $\frac{1}{4} \times \frac{1}{2} = \frac{1}{8}$

An eighth note with one slash would be two sixteenth notes.

A quarter note with two slashes would be four sixteenth notes. You can multiply the bottom number by four: $\frac{1}{4} \times \frac{1}{4} = \frac{1}{16}$

An eighth note with two slashes would be four 32nd notes.

A quarter note with three slashes would be eight 32nd notes.

This is the notation for a buzz roll. Make sure you are able to produce 3 or more bounces per stroke. Push the stick into the drum head to make the bounces faster.

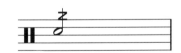

Let's cover different stroke rolls. We'll first take a look at the tremolo markings, which is the way these rolls usually appear. After that, we'll explore a written-out version for better understanding. We will also see ties. "Ties" are the "⌣" markings you'll see in the next section. They look the same as "slurs". A "slur" is when different pitches are smoothly played one into the other, where as a "tie" is the continuation of a previous note and is the same pitch. "Slurs" are not used for snares as they are single-pitched instruments.

5 Stroke Roll

R   R   L   L   R R L L R   L L R R L

6 Stroke Roll

R   L   R   L   L   R   R   R   L L R R L   L   R R L L R

7 Stroke Roll

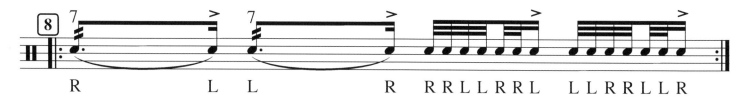

R   L   L   R   R R L L R R L   L L R R L L R

9 Stroke Roll

R   R   L   R   R R L L R R L L R   L L R R L L R R L

10 Stroke Roll

R   R L   L   L R   R R L L R R L L R L   L L R R L L R R L R

Single Stroke Four

R L R L   R L R L   L R L R   L R L R

Single Stroke 7

R L R L R L R   L R L R L R L

35

Triple Stroke Roll

R R R L L L R R R L L L   L L L R R R L L L R R R

Flam

For flams, the hand playing the smaller note will start closer to the head of the drum, while the main note will start higher up.

L R   R L

Flam Accent

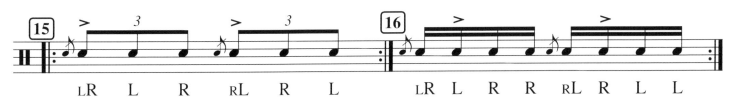

L R L R   R L R L

Flam Paradiddle

L R L R R   R L R L L

Flam Tap

L R   R   R L   L   L R   R   R L   L

Flamacue

L R L R L L R   R L R L R R L

Swiss Army Triplet

L R R L L R R L   R L L R R L L R

Drag

When playing a drag, the trickiest thing is making sure the primary note is on the beat. The proceeding ghost notes should be played before the beat.

L L R   R R L

Single Drag Tap
Single Ratamacue

LLR　L　RRL　R

LLR L R　RRL R L

LLRLRL　RRLRLR

Single Dragadiddle

Is played as

RR L R R　LL R L L

Drag Paradiddle #1

Double Ratamacue

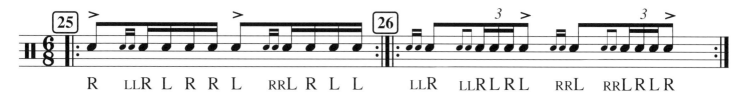

R　LLR L R R L　RRL R L L

LLR　LLRLRL　RRL　RRLRLR

Let's have some fun with rudiments. Try these examples then come up with some of your own!
Double Stroke Roll beat

R R L L R R L L R R L L R R L L　R R L L R R L L R R L L R R L L

Paradiddle beat/fill

R L R R L R L L R L R R L R L L　R L R R L R L L R L R R L R L L

Flam Accent/Swiss Army Triplet fill

LR　L　R　RLL L R RLL L R　LR　L　R　RLL L R RLL L R

Double Ratamacue fill

5 Stroke Roll beat

Note: We generally do not count 32nd notes and count each pair of doubles as a 16th.

If the above is tricky, try this exercise below. It is the same beat but written as 16th and 8th notes which might be easier to read.

Bell Patterns

For this page, play the accents on the bell of the ride. Try these on the hi-hat with accents played with open hi-hat.

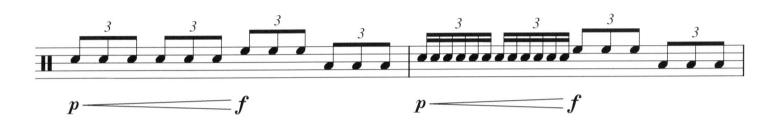

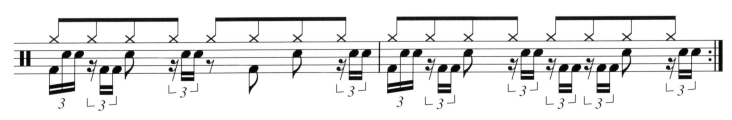

40

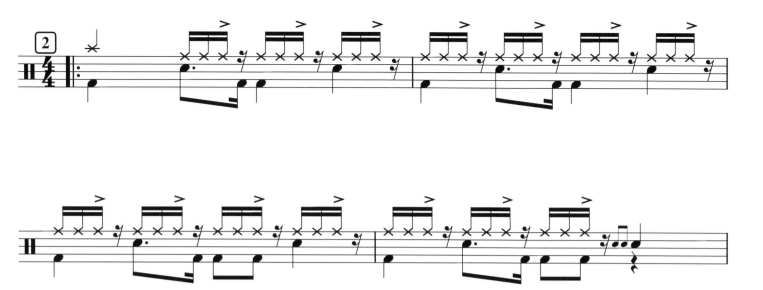

LR R rL L lR R rL L lR

LLR L R rrL R L LR

LR R rL L lR R rL L lR

LLR L R rrL R L LR

Genres

The following section is designed to assist you in understanding fundamental rhythmic patterns within a few popular genres. Many genres have dedicated books about their unique styles due to their rich history and varied rhythms. If there is a genre you want to be proficient in, I recommend doing further research.

Pop

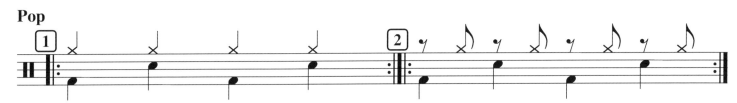

When the bass drum plays all 4 quarter notes, that is called "4 on the floor".

Rock

Country music often uses shuffles and pop beats. A distinctly Country beat is the train beat as seen below. Alternate hands on snare.

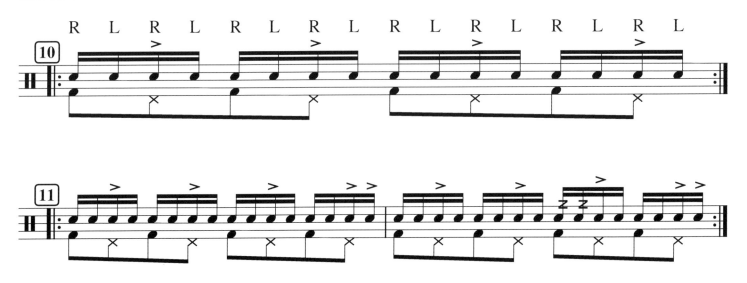

42

Funk

"A little less jazzy, a little more nasty" - Jean-Paul Builes of the band, *REPOSADO*

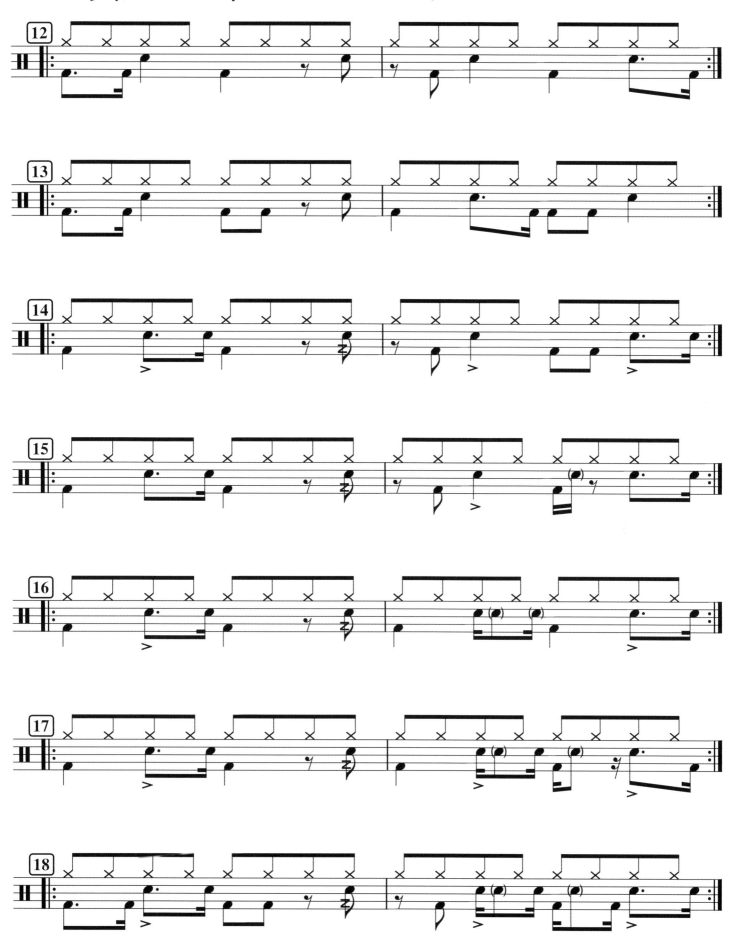

Hip-hop has a lot of funk drums sampled and slowed down.
Try slowing down the funk beats from before to come up with some cool hip-hop beats.

Modern hip-hop beats are programmed and have interesting patterns. Here's an example below.

Drum and Bass because it's fun and why not.

Blues

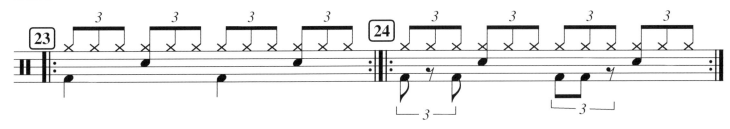

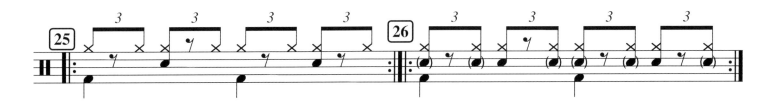

Jazz

In jazz, the cymbal pattern is crucial.
Start with the ride pattern, then add the hi-hat pedal in.

It is common to play a "feathered" (soft dynamic) bass drum on the beat.

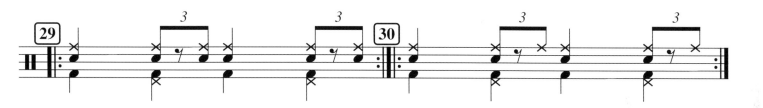

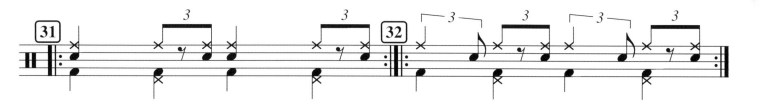

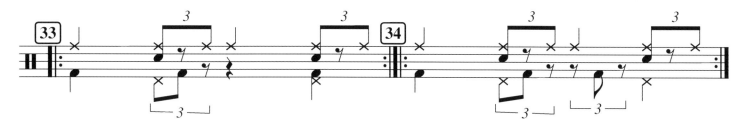

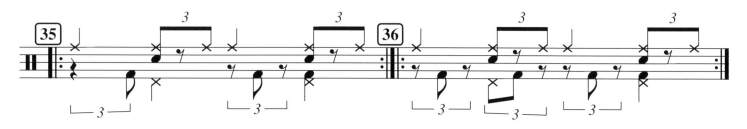

Let's add some fills.

After becoming comfortable with these examples, try improvising some snare and bass patterns. Books such as *Advanced Techniques for the Modern Drummer* by Jim Chapin and *The Art of Bop Drumming* by John Riley are recommended for jazz chops.

46

Latin drumming can be challenging, but the payoff is worth it! Contemporary music is heavily influenced by Latin rhythms, yet many drummers neglect this style in their playing. Go slow and enjoy the ride. Try practicing first with a regular snare hit and switch out for a cross-stick when you're comfortable. The ability to play cross-stick is especially important for bossa nova and samba.

I recommend checking out Tim Haley's website, listed on the appendix. His Latin music material is a great resource.

Samba and Bossa Nova

Let's start with samba feet.
Add the ride after getting comfortable with the feet.

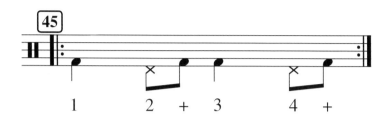

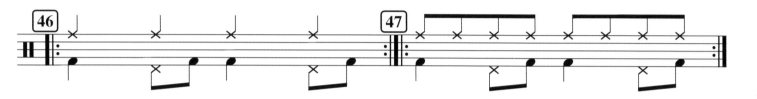

A **clave** is both an instrument and a rhythmic pattern. Like a fun metronome, they keep time for the ensemble.

Son Clave

3 - 2

2 - 3

Let's add the ride and feet!

Rumba Clave

3 - 2

2 - 3

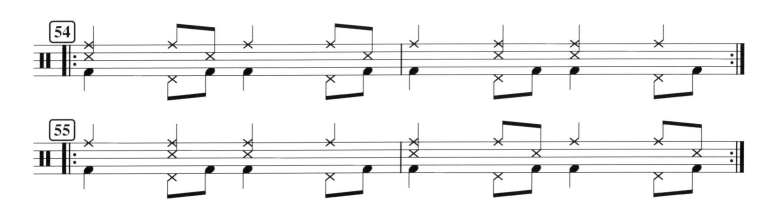

In **Bossa Nova**, you often hear a variation of the Son Clave. Instead of the 3, the + of 3 is played. Some Bossa Nova will omit the 2 and 4 on the hi hat. For practice purposes, we will keep the 2 and 4 on the hi hat.

3 - 2

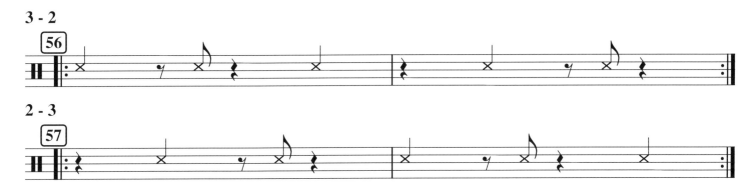

2 - 3

Since Bossa Nova is slower, let's add some eighth-note ride.

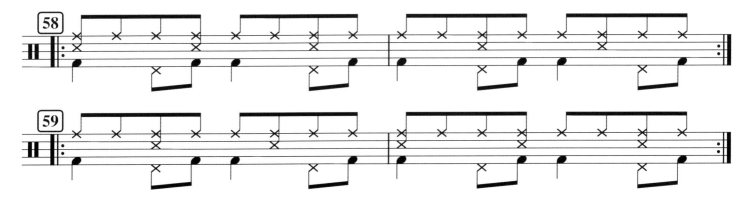

Let's practice being comfortable playing samba feet while soloing.

8th note motifs.

16th note motifs.

49

Reggae

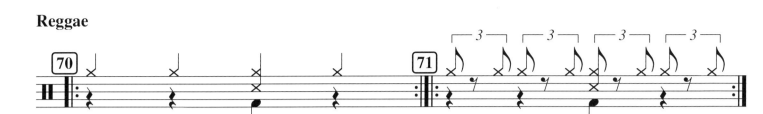

Calypso and **Soca** beats are found in all styles of music! Calypso tends to be a little slower and soca (soul calypso) tend to be more upbeat. Try it with a regular snare then cross stick. Remember to simplify first! You can add the open hi hat when you feel comfortable with the rest of the beat.

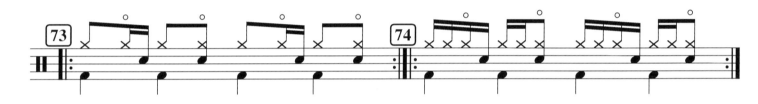

For the **Cha-Cha**, in the second pattern we add a buzzed hi-hat to emulate a güiro.

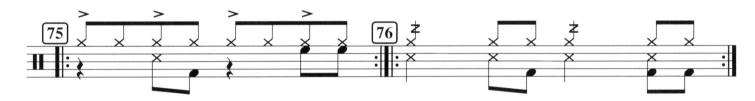

For **Mambo**, you can play the ride pattern on the bell of the ride which is notated by the below diamonds. If you have a cowbell, go ahead and use that for the bell pattern.

We will cover the 6/8 **Bembé/Nanigo** pattern in the next chapter, "Time Signatures."

Time Signatures

So far, we have looked at a time signature called 4/4, which is common in Western music. In this 4/4 time, we count four beats in each measure, and each beat is a quarter note. Typically, counting quarter notes is called "Simple time." "Simple time" is when beats are grouped in twos.

On the other hand, we have "Compound time," where we count eigth notes. In this case, the time signature often looks like 6/8 or 9/8, meaning we count six or nine beats in a measure. But here's the twist: we group these beats into threes.

So, in "Simple time," we count 1-2, 1-2, 1-2, 1-2. In "Compound time," we count 1-2-3, 1-2-3, 1-2-3. Different time signatures can create unique rhythms and feelings in music.

Now, let's check out some other time signatures.

2/4 - 2 quarter notes per measure. You're most likely to see this used as a turnaround in a song.
Example:

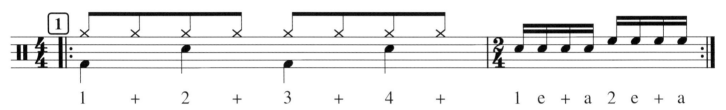

3/4 - Waltz is commonly in 3/4.
Simple waltz   Jazz waltz

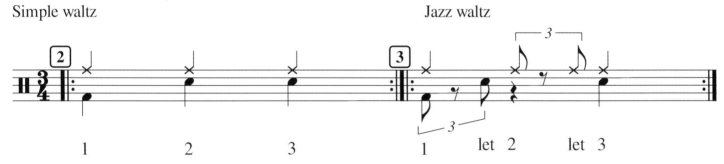

12/8 - Remember to count the eighth notes in these examples.
These grooves are often heard in Blues.

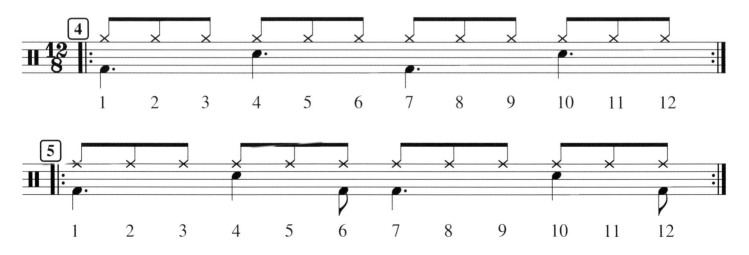

51

6/8 - An excellent example of 6/8 time is the Bembé/Nanigo pattern

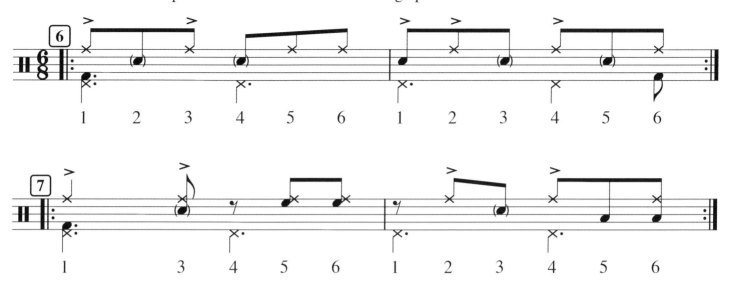

"Odd time signatures" are less common time signatures such as (but not limited to!):

5/4

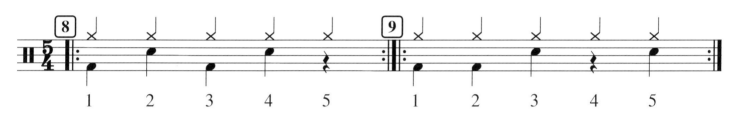

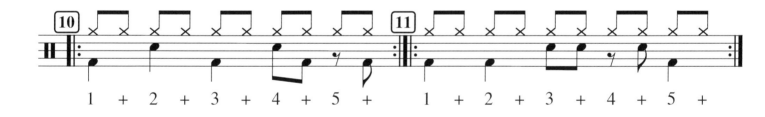

7/4

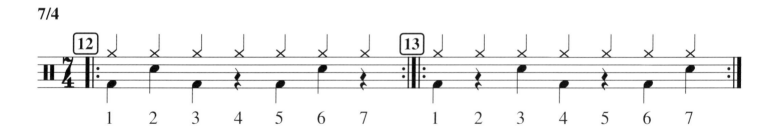

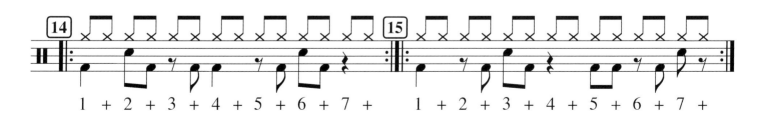

7/8

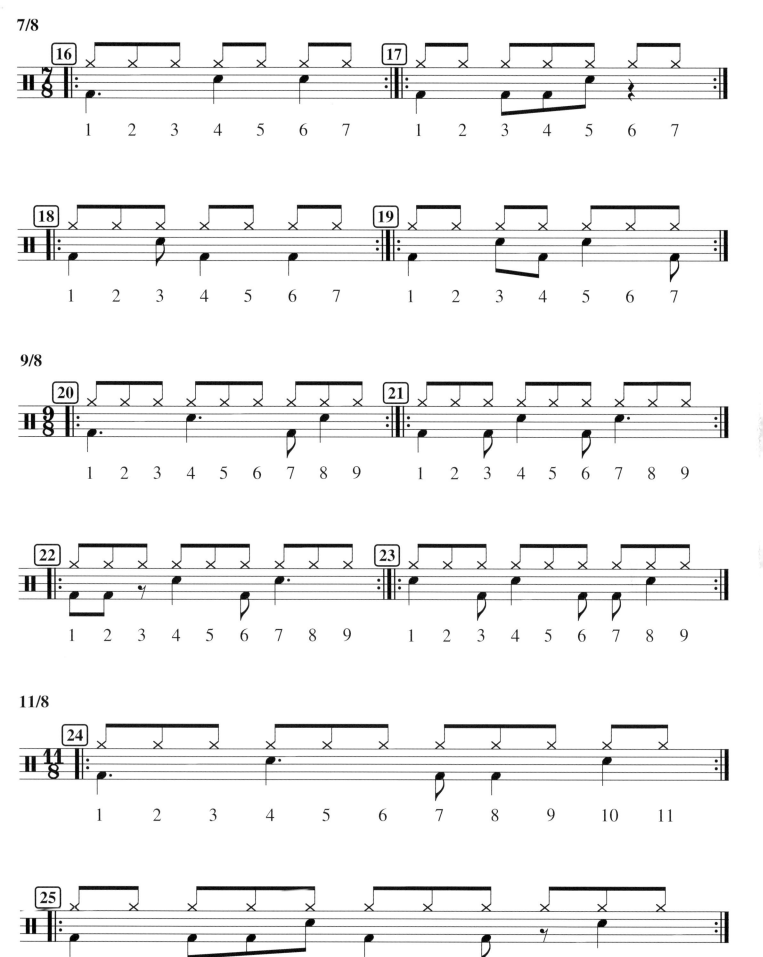

9/8

11/8

53

Blank measures for note taking

Appendix:

Printable PDF and playable Musescore page of book:
https://sites.google.com/view/drum-book-by-nozomi/home

Drumeo has a website and YouTube channel with great content. Two amazing technique videos are:

"Triple Your Hand Speed On The Drums"
Link - https://www.youtube.com/watch?v=r60tW8ZFvtg&t=712s

"Heel-Toe Bass Drum Technique"
Link -https://www.youtube.com/watch?v=xHqkxHaQ-bI&t=56s

Percussive Arts Society has the international drum rudiments listed with audio:
https://www.pas.org/resources/rudiments

Tim Haley has a fantastic website with many different scores of different exercises on genres:
https://drumsettips.org/

For cool visualizations of beats, check out **Drumset Fundamentals** on YouTube:
https://www.youtube.com/@DrumsetFundamentals

Made in United States
Troutdale, OR
03/26/2024

18743132R00031